TRICERATOPS

by Harold T. Rober

BUMBA BOOKS™

LERNER PUBLICATIONS ◆ MINNEAPOLIS

Note to Educators:

Throughout this book, you'll find critical thinking questions. These can be used to engage young readers in thinking critically about the topic and in using the text and photos to do so.

Lerner Publications Company
A division of Lerner Publishing Group, Inc.
241 First Avenue North
Minneapolis, MN 55401 USA

For reading levels and more information, look up this title at www.lernerbooks.com.

Library of Congress Cataloging-in-Publication Data

Names: Rober, Harold T.
Title: Triceratops / by Harold T. Rober.
Description: Minneapolis : Lerner Publications, [2017] | Series: Bumba books. Dinosaurs and prehistoric beasts | Audience: Age 4–8. | Audience: K to Grade 3. | Includes bibliographical references and index.
Identifiers: LCCN 2016019322 (print) | LCCN 2016023330 (ebook) | ISBN 9781512426427 (lb : alk. paper) | ISBN 9781512429169 (pb : alk. paper) | ISBN 9781512427363 (eb pdf)
Subjects: LCSH: Triceratops—Juvenile literature. | Dinosaurs—Juvenile literature.
Classification: LCC QE862.O65 R6227 2017 (print) | LCC QE862.O65 (ebook) | DDC 567.915/8—dc23

LC record available at https://lccn.loc.gov/2016019322

Manufactured in the United States of America
1 – VP – 12/31/16

Expand learning beyond the printed book. Download free, complementary educational resources for this book from our website, www.lerneresource.com.

Table of Contents

Triceratops Had Horns

Triceratops was a kind of dinosaur.

It lived millions of years ago.

It is extinct.

Triceratops was huge.

It was as big as an elephant.

Triceratops lived

in groups.

This helped keep it safe.

Why do you think groups helped keep Triceratops safe?

Triceratops had three horns. Two horns were above its eyes. One was near its nose.

Sometimes Tyrannosaurus rex attacked! Triceratops used its horns to fight.

What else do you think triceratops used its horns for?

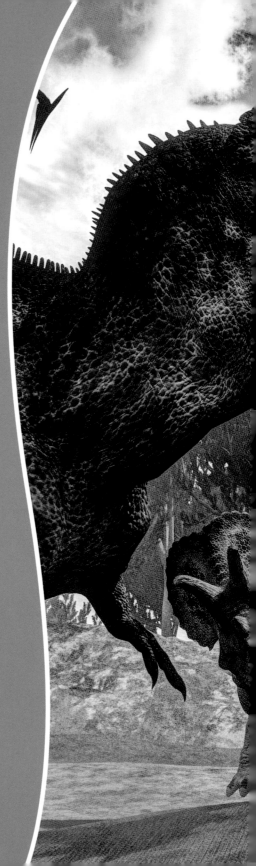

Triceratops had a large frill.

This was a hard bone

behind its head.

The frill may have helped

triceratops stay warm.

Triceratops walked on four legs. Its back legs were long. Its front legs were short.

What other dinosaurs walked on four legs?

beak

Triceratops did
not eat meat.

It ate only plants.

It used its beak to pull

plants out of the ground.

Triceratops had hundreds of teeth.

These teeth had different parts.

The parts made it easy

to chew plants.

Parts of a Triceratops

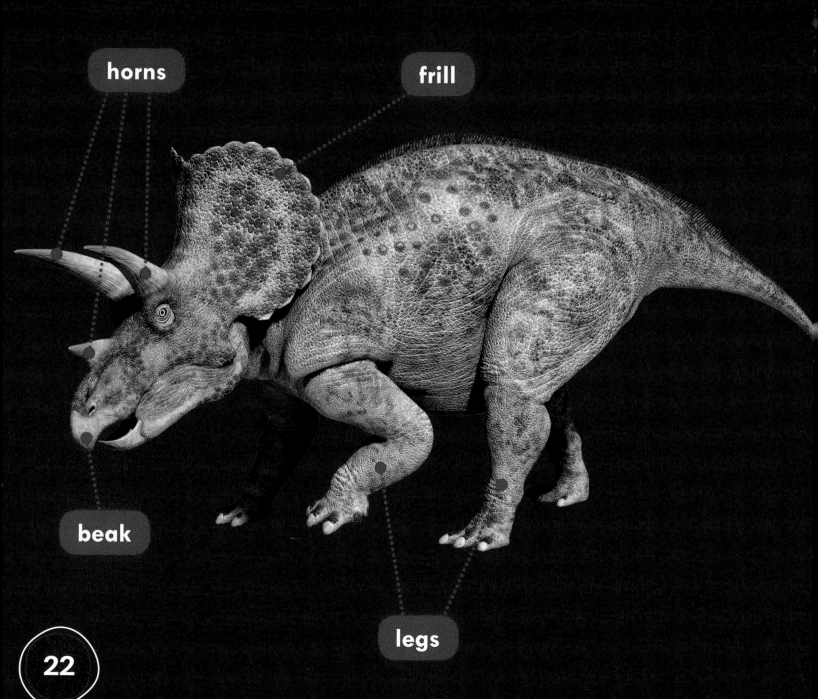

horns

frill

beak

legs

Picture Glossary

beak

the hard, pointed mouth of an animal

extinct

no longer alive

frill

a hard bone behind the head

horns

hard, pointed growths on an animal

Index

Read More

Gray, Susan H. *Triceratops.* Mankato, MN: Child's World, 2015.

Rober, Harold T. *Pterodactyl.* Minneapolis: Lerner Publications, 2017.

Silverman, Buffy. *Can You Tell a Triceratops from a Protoceratops?*
    Minneapolis: Lerner Publications, 2014.

Photo Credits